T0064317

When the Love Affair is Over

A Story of a Love Lost and Found

BJ Hill

WESTBOW®
PRESS
A DIVISION OF THOMAS NELSON
& ZONDERVAN

Copyright © 2015 BJ Hill.

All rights reserved. No part of this book may be used or reproduced by
any means, graphic, electronic, or mechanical, including photocopying,
recording, taping or by any information storage retrieval system
without the written permission of the publisher except in the case
of brief quotations embodied in critical articles and reviews.

WestBow Press books may be ordered through booksellers or by contacting:

WestBow Press
A Division of Thomas Nelson & Zondervan
1663 Liberty Drive
Bloomington, IN 47403
www.westbowpress.com
1 (866) 928-1240

Because of the dynamic nature of the Internet, any web addresses or
links contained in this book may have changed since publication and
may no longer be valid. The views expressed in this work are solely those
of the author and do not necessarily reflect the views of the publisher,
and the publisher hereby disclaims any responsibility for them.

Any people depicted in stock imagery provided by Thinkstock are
models, and such images are being used for illustrative purposes only.
Certain stock imagery © Thinkstock.

ISBN: 978-1-4908-7446-3 (sc)
ISBN: 978-1-4908-7447-0 (e)

Library of Congress Control Number: 2015905133

Print information available on the last page.

WestBow Press rev. date: 07/28/2015

Contents

Prologue

I am looking at the clock. It is 4:40 p.m. In twenty minutes, I'll get to see him. I'll get to see my friend.

He is always there—understanding me, caring for me. He *never* raises his voice. I laugh at myself when he's around. He's not a talker, but there's a calm when he's here.

I watch the clock, hoping that time will fly by and I'll be magically whisked away. It's only four forty-five. Did my watch stop? It's only been five minutes? No way! Still quarter to five. Can't this day go any faster?

We meet when I'm lonely, hurt, sad. He satisfies my needs. I guess I should introduce him. My love is Food.

Food in all shape and sizes. I'm fond of Chinese, Italian, and Mexican Food, and the all-American hoagie. Häagen-Dazs is a favorite. There are things *HD* does to me that give me *mmmm ...no words.* I lick a spoonful of butter pecan; the creamy rich flavor of the ice cream moves to the back of my throat, my toes curl, and my eyes roll back in my head. I experience a moment of complete silence. There aren't words to express how much I love my time with Food.

Whether I'm happy, mad, glad, or sad, there is a food for every emotion. When I'm sad and lonely, a bucket of chicken reminds me of home and the love and warmth I received there.

Angry, I enjoy a whole pizza with sausage, onions, peppers, and mushrooms. The tang of the sauce and spice of the peppers kick my palate like a punch in the face, and I want to hit back.

Happiness is hoagies. Nothing could beat having a day in which all goes well, every deadline is met, and everyone is happy because I delivered sooner than later. My day ends with a whole Italian sub, sometimes turkey and cheese. An unusually-great day, pastrami and swiss with spicy mustard, grilled ...oh please, somebody stop me!

I didn't apologize for entertaining Food in my life. I regarded Food as comfort. That was a long time ago .... Back then I didn't apologize ....

Chapter 1

I was standing at the podium, my head down, gathering the pages of my life. I shared my story. My head was spinning. Sweat rolled down my temple despite the blasting breeze of the air conditioner. My body was shaking with anxiety. I lifted my head and saw people looking directly at me, smiles on their faces and cheers coming from their mouths. There were women crying and men with tears in their eyes. With my heart beating out of my chest, I raised my hands toward heaven. Their applause, cheers, and outpouring of love overwhelmed me. After the applause subsided, the host of this recovery meeting in Fort Lauderdale made final announcements and closed the session.

At the end of the meeting, people stood in line to shake my hand and hug me. Many women in line repeated the same thing: "It happened to me, too."

They shook my hand and whispered, "Your story is powerful, so moving and life changing!" My spirit free and weightless, I floated to my car. Another steamy south Florida night. Winds were mild, the temperature was eighty-two degrees, and the moon was bright and high in a cloudless sky. Behind the wheel, I dropped the top and cruised home wondering how I had gotten here. I remembered when I weighed 358 pounds. I was less than half that size now. Why did I have so much internal pain?

Chapter 2

When I was alone and the apartment was completely silent, it would happen. I'd begin to daydream. Maybe it was the aroma of roasted chicken with all the spices that filled the hallway of my apartment building. It could have been the noise from the street I heard through the front room window. Maybe it was the police sirens or the beeping bus at the corner stop as it lowered steps for passengers to climb aboard. I remembered dreams in my early years. During my twenties, sometimes when I was alone I would see shadows and experience recurring nightmares. Back then I couldn't figure out why. That was years ago. I was sitting on the sofa in my apartment when the daydream started.

I couldn't see faces, only shadows. I saw toys I had played with when I was four years old: a toy train, alphabet blocks, my favorite dolly in her pink dress. I was experiencing a continuous rewind and playback of emotions. When the dream started out, wherever I was, everything fit into place. I trusted this place. I was comfortable. It was a warm, safe feeling.

There was a hint of aftershave in the air. I was standing. A hand moved over my body, touching my lower parts. My body quivered at the touch of his fingers. A sensation I never felt before ran through me. My heart beat faster and faster. I was breathing louder and harder. I tried to speak but couldn't. A moan escaped my lips. I was trembling and lightheaded.

I heard a voice. "You can't say anything. Do you understand? If you tell anyone, you'll get a beating, BJ," the voice insisted.

I didn't understand. Fear overwhelmed me.

Why was I crying?

I heard the same voice. "You want something to eat? I'll make you a sandwich; you will feel better."

What were these dreams about? Who said those things? Why were the dreams so intense? Why? I went inward and tears rolled down my face. What was the fear?And why today was I, a grown woman in the living room of my fifth-floor art deco apartment, suddenly hungry for a sandwich? Not just any sandwich—an American cheese, tomato, and Miracle Whip sandwich on white bread. *Mouth watering!* I walked to the kitchen, opened the refrigerator, and there were the fixings to make the perfect sandwich. As I ate, the fear slipped away. Of course, food calmed me.

More than ten years earlier, I attempted to get answers from friends and relatives. But met with such doubt and unbelief that I shut down.

I could still hear the argument.

There was food cooking on the stove. I could bearly see the top of the stove I could have been around 4 or 5 not yet 6 years old. I smelled gravy simmering, the rice pot boiling.

"What?" they yelled. "What are you talking about?

I was grabbed by both arms and my body was lifted in the air and shaken. I couldn't speak. I was afraid. My lips were numb.

What had I said wrong? Why were they so mad?

"It's all a dream, BJ, just a dream. Do you hear me? Nothing happened."

My body was released, a hand was around my throat.

I struggled to breath. I was sweating, forcing air into my lungs. The grip tightened.

I was lightheaded.

Fingers grabbed my lips, pinching them together—tighter, tighter.

My eyes were firmly shut from fear.

The hand gripping my neck opened.

I heard crying. I began to cry.

I leaned against the wall and slid to the floor, feeling alone and abandoned.

There was pain in my stomach, and I was weak from fear. I wanted to throw up. I lay on the floor balled up with my knees touching my forehead.

I didn't talk to anyone about the dream, ever again.

Chapter 3

For as long as I can remember, all the family and friends from different states would drive or fly south, meeting at the hotel. And then, we meet at the house for a fish fry, barbacue, or cookout.

On this particular occasion, it was a hot summer. I was about six years old we gathered together for fun and good times.

When we arrived, tents and chairs were already set up. The weather was mild, the sun high in the sky, and a warm breeze was in the air. There was nothing but space in the country.

My cousin had a huge backyard with plenty of room for all the family.

The grills were heating up. Big June was seasoning the fish and hamburgers. The hot dogs were ready to be put on the grill. There was always a card table and bar. Bro Man would bring a cooler filled to the brim with beer. His brother had a brown bag in the trunk of his car. Their friends would gather their foldup chairs around the trunk and listen to James Brown, Otis Redding, James Taylor, and others. We could never have a cookout without a talent show. They would all try to outsing each other. These were fun times: folks eating, people laughing, children playing. Life was good.

The children were called to come wash hands and prepare for dinner. I lagged behind—the last one to wash. I took my time getting to the table.

At the dinner table, I sat staring at the plate of food in front of me. "Aren't you hungry?" my cousin asked.

I heard footsteps. I smelled lavender and cigarette smoke.

"You have come a long way baby. You have to eat your food. You need your strength," the raspy voice said.

Mom never made me eat my food if I wasn't hungry.

The kids finished their food and went outside to play. Before leaving the kitchen my cousin said, "Ma'am wants you to eat. Eat your food fast and come outside, please. I'm waiting for you." Ma'am was a family friend who had been with the family for years and had raised a lot of us and was always around at the family gatherings.

I picked up the spoon held it in my hand. "Ma'am," I said, "I'm not hungry right now. May I go outside?"

"We eat all our food in this house," she answered. "You must eat before you go outside."

I began to cry. The voice demanded, "Eat your food now!"

She took the spoon from my hand, filled it with food, and forced it into my mouth. I was paralyzed with fear. I couldn't chew.

"Child, if you don't chew your food, your butt will burn! You will take off all your clothes. Do you want that?" she asked.

I shook my head no. But I still couldn't chew. She slowly walked into the kitchen and returned with a belt that hung on the wall on a hook near the stove. She gave me a whack across my thigh with the belt.

"Chew your food now. I mean it."

The sting from the belt made tears roll down my face, but my mouth couldn't move. My jaws were frozen. She hit me again across my back. I began to weep and chew.

"Shut it up and eat," she said. That's good food we don't waste food around here.

I chewed. She put another spoonful of food to my lips. I didn't chew or swallow. She held up the belt for me to see. I began to chew. There was another spoon with food to my lips. Ma'am pushed the spoon into my mouth, forcing the food already in my mouth to the back of my throat. I gagged and threw up all the food on the floor.

She yelled, "What is wrong with you? You're throwing up all that good food!"

There was hamburger and hot dog all over me and her new linoleum floor. She grabbed me and threw me against the wall.

"Get every drop of food off my new floor!" she shouted. She smacked me in the face. "Look at this! Get up this mess!" she barked.

Terrified, I began to sob. I was crying but not making a sound. I couldn't breathe. I couldn't move. I was catatonic.

Family members heard the ruckus and came to see. "What's going on?" I heard. "What happen?"

"Y'all go on back outside. The child spilled her food. She's got to get up her mess. She'll be outside in a minute." "Ma'am, can I help?" my cousin asked.

"No," Ma'am yelled, "Y'all go on out so she can get up her mess. She's fine." Ma'am brought newspapers and a pale for me to get up the food and a mop for the floor.

No matter whose table I sat, hungry or not, I ate all the food on my plate. I doubled in size within three months.

Chapter 4

I was nine years old. After school, a bunch of us kids walked to the corner candy store where everyone got his or her favorite treat. I walked through the store, waiting, watching, and sniffing to see if something would entice me. There were bright colors and intriguing wrappers, dancing candies, and smiling candies. I smelled the grape, strawberry, and watermelon flavors of the Now & Laters. I saw a talking candy display. After their purchases, my friends gathered to show off their delectable delicacies. Each day, I walked out, uninterested. The others ooohed and ahhed as they traded candy and shared their sugary experiences. One day, I decided not to go into the store with my friends. I just didn't get the same excitement they did in the sweets.

I stood outside the store to discover an aroma I wasn't sure of. It was magically alluring and captivating! At first whiff, I leaned my head back, my nose up in the air. I followed the scent.

"Where are you going?" my friend Jamie asked.

I waved her off and turned toward the smell. I walked two blocks and around the corner. The scent grew stronger and stronger until I found myself in front of Vinny's Pizzeria. Heaven! I'm from north Newark, New Jersey. The aromas from my mother's kitchen were fried chicken and collard greens. We lived between Puerto Rican and Italian neighborhoods. Rice and beans from one side of the block and pasta and red tomato sauce from the other. I entered Vinny's Pizzeria and saw two men behind the counter. Both were covered with sprinkles of white flour and wearing hats like Chef Boyardee. I attended grammar school across town, riding public transportation to get there. There were no pizzerias in my neighborhood.

"Hey, I'm Tony," one of the men said. "Would you like a slice?"

"A slice?" I said. "What's a slice?"

Before I knew it, a beautiful, well-rounded woman with a checkered apron, wonderful flowing black hair, and gorgeous brown eyes said, "Oh my goodness, you don't know what a slice is?" She was beautiful and chubby like me.

"No," I answered. Then she said words that warmed my heart. "Tony, get the kid a slice."

I stood behind the glass display watching Tony open the oven door. I felt the heat hit my face as I stood on my tippy toes anticipating a slice coming to greet me. Tony used a long stick with a paddle on the end of it. In slow motion, the pizza slid from the oven to a silver plate on the counter. The steam fogged the glass. The aroma was all I could imagine. I'd arrived.

My mouth watered as he used a tool to cut the pie across. He pulled the pieces apart from the circle and put one on a paper plate.

"Are you ready for the best-tasting slice in the whole world?" he asked.

"Yes, yes!" I replied impatiently.

Still standing on my toes, Tony gracefully handed me the plate. I couldn't take my eyes off the slice. I slowly walked to a corner table so my slice and I could get better acquainted.

I was intrigued by the way the slice was shaped, and how the cheese gently melted over the sauce. I marvelled at how the crust was slightly brown on the top. Some of the cheese slid off the slice and onto the plate. With my finger I gently lifted some excess cheese with a hint of sauce. I tasted the basil, garlic, tomatoes, and a flavor of cheese I'd never experienced. My taste buds were awakened. At home, we ate Kraft American cheese—good cheese, just not mozzarella.

Tony yelled, "Stop looking at the slice! Pick it up, fold the crust with one hand, take a bite of the other side."

He had no idea of the repercussions and how this slice would affect my life.

At first bite, I was in love—and the affair began. I still walked with my school chums to the candy shop. But I kept walking to Vinny's Pizzeria.

The hard days were over now. I had found a friend.

Chapter 5

Every day after school I would go to Vinny's for a slice. After a while my palate needed something new—more excitement. I was ready to go exploring for more food that would fit the bill.

It was Monday, another eighth-grade school day like any other ordinary day. When I arrived at school, my girlfriend Cynthia was handing out her birthday invitations. Everyone talked about who she would invite. No one knew what day or time the event would be. When Cynthia approached me, she smiled and handed me a beautiful pink envelope with yellow, pink, and green flowers on the front next to my name. I wanted to jump up and scream. *Yeah, she picked me!* I hugged her and said thank you. My first junior high school party! What? This was my first party ever.

After school, I gave my mom the invitation and asked her if I could go. She said yes.

Cynthia's house was wonderfully decorated. There were colorful blue, yellow, and pink balloons and streamers. Music was playing in the background. Of course, the Temptations, Marvin Gaye, Aretha Franklin, and the Four Tops were some of the entertainment.

Cynthia's mother displayed a wonderful designer five-piece serving tray that swiveled around. It held chips, dip, popcorn, pretzels, and cheese doodles. *Get out of town! Somebody stop me.* I knew there was music, but I didn't care where it was coming from; my eyes were fixated on the wonderful revolving serving dish. I loved the taste of the pretzels and potato chips together. I tried cheese doodles and corn chips. My first experience with chips and dip was heaven. Nothing else mattered. The serving dish captured my attention. But what was *in* the dish kept me there—the flavors, the shapes, the crisp smell of cheese doodles. The crunch of the pretzels. I was a plump child, and Mom didn't allow these kinds of snacks in our house—a great reason to run away from home.

Chapter 6

I lived in a multicultural neighborhood: Hispanics, Italians, and African Americans. In high school, I was among the larger girls. Everyone was slim, wearing sizes four, six, eight,and ten—ten being the largest, outside of me, of course.

The girls were petite with long flowing hair. They were gorgeous. I didn't fit in.

My mom shopped at Lane Bryant for my clothes. I didn't dress like the other girls. I wore tent dresses and jumpers with blouses.

The girls wore pedal pushers, hip huggers, midriff tops, ponytails, and sneakers no larger than a size five.

I rarely saw any of them in the cafeteria. If they were there, they were meeting each other *in front of* the cafeteria during lunch period to walk together to the schoolyard during lunch period.

The boys from the neighborhood came to the school during lunch to meet up with girls. I attended an all-girls school, and the boys school was a few blocks away.

One afternoon during lunch period, my friend Maria invited me to go outside with some other girls to flirt with the boys.

"Come on," she said, "you only sit here, eat, and go back to class. Let's go get some air."

"I don't want to go out there, Maria. Those girls don't like me," I said.

"Who cares who those girls like or don't like? They don't own the schoolyard. We don't have to go over by them anyway."

Gloria, with whom Maria usually ate lunch, was absent from school that day. Maria needed a *wing man* to walk with her around the schoolyard. The girls all lined up at the fence waiting for the boys to come over to say hi.

At first, I was excited. Everybody was out there.

Some were jumping rope, others were playing dodge ball or running bases to see who was the fastest.

I had never seen them laughing, talking, and playing. I'd only seen them in class.

I was afraid Maria wanted to play one of the activities. I was not up for it.

No one outside of my gym class had ever seen me run or waddle.

"Wow," I said. "Everyone is out here."

"I told you," Maria said. "See what you're missing?"

Someone threw the dodge ball so hard it came across the schoolyard. I ran after the ball and threw it back to the players; a part of me wished to join the game. I still couldn't believe I had run for that ball.

"There's Hector," she said.

"Who is Hector?" I asked.

"He's the boy I go to the movies with Saturdays."

"Wow, your mom lets you go to the movies with a boy?" I said.

"Don't you go?" Maria asked.

"Not really," I said. "We're always in church."

We walked across the schoolyard. The closer we got to the fence, the cuter Hector seemed. Maria started smiling. I began to wish it was Hector who was looking for me.

Before we made it to the fence, one of the boys with Hector shouted, "Hey, big momma!"

Maria shouted, "Hey, shut your mouth! You're so stupid. She's with me."

Hector yelled, "Come on, man, what you doing? Don't disrespect."

I ran away. Maria yelled my name. Tears rolled down my face before I made it back inside the school. I never went to the schoolyard at lunchtime again.

I was an outcast. I didn't fit in.

Chapter 7

There was a time in my life when I couldn't live without food—and not just for nutrition. Food was close at hand, near me, next to me.

Food calmed me. Food soothed me. When food was nearby, I felt safe.

Some understood this; others didn't. Some days, I didn't either.

There were days I didn't want to feel.

My emotions were too much for me to handle. My appetite increased, not hunger, but an uncontrollable need to eat.

There were days when I wasn't hungry, and I'd eat two or three sandwiches.

I'd be okay when I knew there was a hoagie or two around—bologna and cheese, turkey and cheese or at least a couple of slices of pound cake neatly wrapped in plastic and a chocolate chip or peanut butter cookie or two.

There would always be cakes and cookies, just in case.

Throughout my high school years, I hid food in my bedroom—sandwiches, cookies, cakes.

No one could possibly understand what was going on in my head. To be honest, neither could I.

During high school, I had a recurring dream of falling off a cliff. I would fall—or someone would throw or push me.

In a deep sleep, I saw an old RCA black-and-white TV in the living room.

A shadow came toward me. I smelled aftershave.

Huge hands came at me. I was picked up by my clothes and thrown through the air, flying from one room into the next. *Bam*! My body slammed against the wall. I bounced onto the bed, crying hysterically. My wrist twisted during the hit. I lay injured on the bed, and again I smelled aftershave. "If you don't stop crying, I'll give you something to cry for."

I always needed something to eat after I relived that dream.

It was lunchtime. I was in the school cafeteria. I used my lunch tickets and got two lunches. I would go through the same routine day-in and day-out, enlisting a couple of girlfriends to get a second lunch for me with their tickets through the lunch program. They didn't care; they were under the impression that I didn't have enough food at home and that second lunch was my dinner—despite the fact that I weighed 170 pounds in my freshman year.

There was enough food in my house. Wherever I saw food I had to have it. I took it home with me. I am not sure how to explain it.

It was my way out. I didn't want to feel the fear. It was unbearable.

In high school, I would wrap turkey and cheese or bologna and cheese sandwiches in plastic wrap to take home. When I arrived home, I would put them in Ziploc bags and hide them in my drawer under my school clothes. Hiding food gave me a sense of control. In the closet, I kept sandwiches in Ziploc bags, in boxes for safekeeping. Under the bed, there were sandwiches wrapped in foil, neatly secured in shoeboxes. When I couldn't sleep, I'd look under the bed to see the boxes. I'd lift the lid, feel inside, and go back to sleep. Hiding food, I felt safe.

I woke up one morning to Mom leaning over me. "It's time to get up, Sweetie!"

"What's wrong?" I asked.

"Why is all this food in your room?" Mom asked. "Where are you getting these sandwiches? Are you stealing them? Is that why you are hiding them? What is going on?"

She began to pull boxes from under the bed, opening drawers and uncovering plastic bags full of sandwiches. She went to the closet and pulled down shoeboxes from the top shelf and asked, "Is there food in these boxes?"

I was afraid to answer.

"Answer me!" she yelled.

"What happened?" I asked. "The commercial said the bags are airtight. There aren't any bugs. Okay?"

Mom let go of a deep sigh, sat on my sister's twin bed, and said, "Come here, baby. It's not about bugs. Why do you need all this food in here? There is food in the kitchen, and whenever you ask, I give you money to get treats. Why are you doing this? Are you saving it for a friend? What is it?"

I almost accepted *saving it for a friend* as the truth to assure her I wasn't crazy. *Yes, the food is for a friend!* But I couldn't bring myself to say it.

After she found the food I'd hid, there was a forty-minute discussion on keeping food where it belongs.

Mom was frustrated and puzzled. There was worry in her voice when we discussed the food. She asked me, "Why? What's wrong? Is there not enough food in the house? Why do you bring food from school and put it in your room?" She gently and tenderly asked, "Is there something you can't tell me?"

But I couldn't put it into words.

"We will get someone to help you, to talk to you," she suggested.

I couldn't look at her, seeing her worry and despair. She wanted to help me, but I couldn't let her. I was caught in a food dilemma.

At high school graduation, I weighed 240 pounds.

Chapter 8

I n college, there was always an excuse for a party: someone's birthday, an exam, a get-together. We all lived within a ten-mile radius of the college we eventually graduated from.

Where there was a party, there was food—all kinds of food. I loved it when everybody would bring his or her favorite dish and we'd all share it. It reminded me of the candy store in Newark where everyone shared their treats. I didn't have a favorite. I loved it all. Mexican? Love it! A barbecue theme? I'd make sure the sauce was hot and spicy. Italian theme? Suzanne from Kentucky made the best lasagna. Mi-Sing— *MiTi* for short—had birthday parties that were the best. There was nonstop Chinese food and the greatest shrimp egg rolls ever made.

I was designated *party location tracker.* We didn't have MapQuest, but I knew the area well. Twenty years earlier, I had lived in Washington, DC for about ten years. I'd give directions with food landmarks— naming restaurants, not streets.

"Two blocks down from Jack in the Box." "When you cross over there is a TGI Fridays …" "Look for the McDonalds.""Remember where the Blimpies is located, right before the rib joint?"

"We went to that place last year. It's right across the street from the restaurant where we had Cynthia's birthday party. It's the building with the beautiful mural, and you said the appetizers were to die for."

I followed my nose.

I'd plan dinner parties around a particular food and invite people to enjoy it.

I wasn't the only thick girl at these events. There were healthy, hefty, big-boned, queen-sized ladies.

I must admit, the size fours, sevens, eights, and tens got the most play at the time. But times were changing.

I wasn't a hater. It was all in fun. There was Glen.

He was a tall drink of water with a smile that lit up a room and dimples to match. He had graduated from Georgetown. I heard he went pre-med.

He always beat me at dominos. He was such a character.

One Friday, we got together at Michele's for our usual and Michele yelled, "Hey, B! Guess who is on his way over?"

"Who?" I asked.

"Glen," she said.

"Why are you telling me?"

"Oh, you know you like him."

"Girl, he is too fine to be a chubby-chaser."

"Well, every time he comes to one of your parties, he's warming up to you, my dear, and no one else." She laughed.

"Really? I never noticed. I'm here for the food."

"I thought you knew."

There was a knock at the door. Michele looked over and smiled at me. "Come here."

"What do you want?" I asked.

She grabbed me, took me to her bedroom, and put makeup on my face. When she was done, she said "Now, look in the mirror. What do you think?"

"Wow," I said. "It doesn't look like me."

"Oh, yes it does. It just enhances your pretty face."

"You mean my fat face? Right?" I laughed.

"Stop being so hard on yourself."

There was a knock at the bedroom door. "Hey, are y'all coming out?"

My stomach flickered. For the first time, I had butterflies in my stomach.

"I don't know what he would think of the new me."

"Girl, let's go get a chicken leg. Who cares what he thinks?"

Michele exited the bedroom first, and I heard his voice.

"Hey, girl, what's up?" Glen asked Michele.

"Same ol' same ol'. B's here. She's in the back."

I couldn't believe she'd done that. Why had she told him I was there?

"What's up, girl, you coming out or what? Afraid I will beat you at dominos?"

Nervously, I walked to the entrance of the bedroom and stood there for a moment. "No, Glen, I'm not afraid of you. I let you win anyway. How about that?"

"Oh really? Let's see that in slow motion." He laughed. "Come out here."

I exited the bedroom.

"You look different. Oh, the makeup is nice. Good color on you."

I couldn't move from the doorway. My hand gripped the door.

He noticed. I felt I was going to pass out.

"Hey," Glen yelled. "Are you going to get the dominos? I have an early day tomorrow. Let me show you how's it's done before I leave."

I got the game. We set up the dominos.

"I like the outfit. Nice." He smiled.

"You finally got a hair cut," I giggled.

"I knew I was coming to see you."

"Okay, here we go. Why do you start with that stuff? You like making jokes," I said.

"I am not joking. You never take me seriously. Will you ever give me a chance?" He stared at me. "No worries. I will win this game, and you will know who's boss."

"You always say that, Glen," I giggled. "Ten years from now, you will say the same thing, and I will show *you* how it's done. Believe that," I winked.

"I can't wait to see that," he said with a smile.

That was the last night I saw Glen. We didn't keep in touch. I heard he went off and became a doctor working with kids, or something like that.

Of course, I blamed it on my weight.

He didn't keep in touch, because I was too fat. I was the big girl nobody could love. Always the friend and never the girlfriend. The boys would say, *that's my home girl, my buddy, my play sister.* Oh, how I hated it when my guy friends would call me their *homey.* "Sup, Homy?" Especially when they were with a cutie. She would be five-feet-three, 105 pounds, with a bright smile, deep dimples and a shape—well, you know.

I wanted to rip her hair out, make her trip, throw her down to the ground. But I didn't.

The boys didn't choose me.

You would never know I was the one they came crying to when life got hard, when they lost a puppy, or when somebody stole their Tonka Truck.

Well, no more. I wasn't going to let that happen again.

Chapter 9

It's said that if you do something long enough, you can become a professional at it. Practice, practice, practice. Well, I'm a professional dieter. You name it, I've tried it! I know all the techniques, tips, and slogans:

Don't eat before 8:00 a.m.

Start your day with protein.

Don't eat after 6:00 p.m., and never after eight p.m. if you had carbs at lunchtime.

Eat your heaviest meal during lunch and don't have carbs at dinner.

Start with a minimum of forty-five minutes of cardio per day."

You have to be thin to win!

Do you know how many diets are out there? I didn't until I made a short list of the plans I had tried:

The liquid diets.

The *eat carbs three days a week and protein the fourth day* plan.

The *eat fruit before anything* diet.

The *take this pill on an empty stomach* diet.

The *take this pill before eating fat and the fat will flush out of your system* diet.

There are others:

Don't count carbs, count calories.

Don't count calories, count carbs.

How much sugar is too much sugar?

Subtract the fiber and sugar from the protein.

How much is too much protein?

Stop all that noise! Where does it all end?

Honestly, who knows the right answers? Whatever the health and fitness magazines tout this week will likely change the next week.

Each diet I attempted occurred at a different time in my life.

I used different diets for different situations, whether it was a wedding, barbecue, office party, vacation, or high school reunion—or just because I felt I could finally do it.

I had dropped twenty pounds so many times, but it was a boomerang—it kept coming back.

I don't know why I kept letting those twenty pounds come back. No matter how many times I attempted to lose the weight, it was like the neighborhood mangy alley cat: feed it once, and it always comes back. It was like an old dress in the back of the closet that I think will come back in style.

Fat never comes in style.

I weighed and measured.

The meals were mailed to my house.

I purchased prepackaged meals at the doctor's office.

There were shots, drinks, bars, seven-day plans, three day plans, and burn-all-the-weight-you-want plans.

Drink this juice and lose weight like the stars.

Follow this plan, and you are guaranteed to lose fifteen pounds in ten days.

The soup diet (the worst)—I was up all night with gas. I burned so much incense people thought I was smoking pot.

There were pills, powders, and the thrills of purchasing new equipment every other month.

I purchased weight equipment and stationary bikes to ride daily.

The exercise videos were so advanced that instead of participating, I went to the store to get snacks and then came back to watch the people in the videos break a sweat.

Here we go again. I purchased the latest and greatest fat-busting exercise video. After fifty minutes of heavy breathing and sweating, I completed the session.

I went to the refrigerator to get some water and grabbed carrot cake instead.

I did learn that when beginning a new plan, it's important to throw out all the old stuff.

Don't get me wrong; it all works. Something works for everybody! However, I realized it wasn't what I was eating that was the problem. It was what was eating at me from the inside.

It didn't matter what I ate or didn't eat—steamed, boiled, fried, or just laid to the side. There were many diets and many lonely nights spent wondering, *Why is this happening to me?*

Chapter 10

I was at my wit's end. I decided surgery was the answer.

The day of surgery, I was thinking, "I'm going to be beautiful." I didn't tell anyone I was going under the knife. I didn't need to hear opinions.

I wanted to look like all the other girls.

I wanted to be normal. I wanted men to *see* me—look at me the way they looked at the other girls.

I was cut open, sectioned, and reconnected like a broken doll.

In the recovery room, I opened my eyes. I couldn't see much. Everything was blurred. I wasn't feeling any pain. The meds hadn't worn off yet. I almost forgot I had just experienced a life-changing surgery. I heard the nurse.

"Hi! You are in the hospital, and you had surgery. Can you hear me?"

"Yes," I whispered.

"You'll be taken back to your room in a few minutes and given some instructions you must follow. When you wake up, you are going to feel quite a bit of pain, but you will have access to medication to help relieve it."

There was no way I was going to eat anything ever again. I fell asleep believing all my dreams had come true.

Early the next morning, I woke up to the most excruciating pain. I could barely breathe. I felt like someone was sitting on my chest stabbing me in the stomach.

"You are going to have to get up every couple of hours and walk for thirty minutes from one end of the hospital floor to the other," the nurse said.

I said, "Does anyone realize I just had surgery?"

Apparently, I had to walk for blood flow. That's when it hit me that I had really had surgery—my stomach cut in the center under my breasts and down to my navel. To lie there was painful enough, but to sit up was worse. They gave me instructions on what to do: I must not do anything to tear the stitches.

Startled, I said, "I have stitches?"

"Well, what did you think you were going to get?" the nurse asked.

"I don't know. I want to look like the other girls." I was in my early forties but sounded naive and uninformed. I was.

I rolled over onto my side and propped myself up, grabbing a chair for balance. I pondered, *What in the world have I done to myself?*

I kept telling myself, "I'm pretty. This is good. I'll look like the other girls."

I was in post-op, barely able to stand.

Who were the other girls I wanted to look like? At that moment, I couldn't remember, and I began to walk from one nurses' station to the other.

I wasn't alone. There were many other women. Some needed nurse assistance to walk.

The hospital smell was unusual to me; I couldn't quite make it out. The nurse put socks on my feet to walk the floor. The floor was freshly waxed, so my socks slid across without getting stuck. I was chilly. I wore two hospital gowns to stay warm. The gowns were rough and itchy rubbing against my skin. I could hear various TV shows from adjacent rooms as I walked the hall. The nurses were at the station watching the patients.

There was Stacy. She walked the hall whispering, "Why did I do this?"

The woman in room 525 said to her daughter, "Oh my, no, I should have thought this out."

I walked down the hall and heard a woman on her cell phone discussing her stay with her friend. "I want this, but I should have waited."

I was in pain. I felt like crying. I said to myself, "It's okay. I will be thin just like the other girls."

I left the hospital. I couldn't eat. I was afraid too much food would tear the pouch. How much was too much?

I lost seventy-five pounds in two months, which was such a sudden lifestyle change. I lost weight so rapidly that the elasticity in my skin was gone. Many people have heard the term *dumping syndrome*. After surgery, when you have sugar that your body can't metabolize, it's called *dumping*. It's hard to explain your body experiences a rise in temperature by several degress you begin to sweat, your vision is blurred and you are lightheaded and have dry mouth. I would have to sit down due to lightheadedness.

Before surgery a physician's assistant discussed issues about excessive drinking. "If you are an alcoholic, stop drinking," he said.

How can you do that?

It was after the surgery I recognized drinking was my issue.

The assistant said, "You will have a pouch, and if you are drinking more than four glasses of wine a day, you will need to scale back. You only need a small amount to feel the effects of liquor. You can cause serious damage if you drink too much."

My research before the surgery was short and limited. It consisted of finding out how many women had the surgery and whether they were successful in losing weight.

I should have looked into how many woman *didn't* do it and why.

I had lost weight so many times before. What would make this different?

I was in the hospital. There were doctors and nurses. Professionals would provide medical care. I could see success on the horizon.

I didn't have the ability to love myself from the inside. I was fixing my body from the outside.

I thought this would make me lovable, likable, and pretty.

Chapter 11

∞

One year out of surgery, I was walking one hundred and twenty pounds lighter. I couldn't believe how I'd changed so quickly.

I was shopping at different stores. In my younger days, I had shopped Lane Bryant, Smart Size, the Answer, and a couple of other queen-size stores. The tent dress and polyester pants had served their purpose.

But I was ready for regular shops and regular sizes.

In the beginning, I was very careful about what I ate—no sugar and no ice cream. I was instructed to eat softer foods, macaroni and cheese and pureed foods, in very small portions. I was so afraid to eat food that I drank protein shakes for a month and a half after the surgery. I was afraid. I wasn't sure what food I might put in my mouth and not be able to stop eating until

I began to bleed or throw up. I was not aware of the triggers.

Woman after woman shared stories with me about how she couldn't stop eating. They ate until they gagged and threw up food—and looked for more food after they'd thrown up. I didn't want that to be a part of my story. I decided on protein shakes and my favorite softer food. I was not tempted to eat my old favorite food until a year after the surgery.

Life was good. I was not stuffing huge amounts of food into my mouth. I could actually go to the supermarket and purchase groceries and not eat my way through them.

I could go to the buffet, see all the different kinds of food—fried rice, ribs, chicken, pizza, green beans, mac and cheese, cake, ice cream—and walk away.

I was in heaven. I had finally arrived. This was it. I knew it. I was just like the other girls. I had finally done it. I was normal.

Shopping was my favorite thing. When I was younger, Mom made shopping a chore. There weren't many *large woman* clothing stores or shops that carried my size. It was different now.

I went home to see Mom, and we went shopping at Macy's. We walked through the store.

Mom looked around and said, "Well, I guess there is no need for you to go to the woman's section. You are way too small for that." She smiled.

Can you imagine? You would have thought I'd hit the Lotto.

I couldn't help but smile and say, "You got that right." I was elated.

I had lost weight, and Mom acknowledged it.

No more comments about being overweight. No more suggestions about which diet I should try. No more hurt feelings, thinking my mother didn't love me because I was fat.

No more tears when someone said, "I am not trying to hurt your feelings, but you ain't gonna find no man being that big. That's just the truth about the matter!"

It didn't matter how true it was; it still hurt.

I was the girl everybody liked now.

But did I like myself?

I began walking and drinking more water. Why? It seemed like the right thing to do. I was one of *those* girls; I did what they did.

It had been almost two years postsurgery. I had now lost two hundred pounds. I hadn't realized carrying the extra weight was like having another person on my back. As a result, I had stayed tired and unmotivated.

Food not being my main focus now, I discovered a new world—or just things I hadn't experienced yet.

I planned a trip out of town.

I could walk through the airport and make it to the next flight without stopping at a Burger King to sit down and rest. *Oh well, since I'm here I can get a quick snack before I get on the next plane.*

I could stand more than ten minutes without agonizing back pain.

When I walked on the plane, people didn't stare at me with *the look*. Oh, you know the look—the *hope I'm not going to sit next to you ruining your trip because you don't have enough room* look.

I could sit in an airplane seat and use only one seatbelt.

My feet had shrunk. I wore smaller-sized shoes, not the same width. I used to wear triple E—not any more.

I was able to pull my car seat closer to the steering wheel.

It really was a different world.

Chapter 12

Three years postsurgery, I decided to go to my favorite Thai restaurant, The Thai House, just to see who might be there to see the new me. I wanted to see what kind of attention my new body would receive. There he was—the most beautiful creature I had ever seen in my life. Six feet two, smooth caramel skin, hazel eyes, black hair, one dimple in his right cheek, and pearly white teeth. He looked familiar. *Don't we always say that. Like you really know him! Maybe in a dream …*

I pretended I didn't see him. I glanced over to see if our eyes would meet, and they did. He was sitting in the front of the restaurant waiting for his order. He came over to my table. My heart leapt. I had asked for a soda while waiting for the order I'd placed.

"Hi. My name is Peter. I have seen you here often before. But you have changed quite a bit since the last time you were here. You look amazing."

I didn't remember seeing him in the restaurant, but it was okay. Someone had noticed! *No way is this happening to me. Oh, it's a good day!*

"I am interested in knowing what you did to lose all that weight," he asked.

"Of course," I said. "You know the basics—fewer carbohydrates and fat and more exercise." I never ever told anyone I had the surgery, because they would think I was weak. People don't know all the pain involved.

Peter looked at me from head to toe.

"Well, it really worked for you. Congratulations."

He reached out to hug me. *A little forward*, I thought. But at that moment, in his arms, nothing else mattered. I was one of *the girls*. It was worth it.

I was so lost in him, how he smelled and the strength of his body as he stepped toward me. I found myself slightly leaning in for more, and he laughed.

I played it off. "What is that awesome cologne?" I went in for another whiff.

He looked deep into my eyes and said, "You like that, huh? I wasn't sure it would get attention. But now that I have yours, I guessed it worked."

I smiled. *Oh, yeah, buddy. It worked, all right. And you can work me anytime.* My Christian values, everything Mom, Dad, and Auntie had said—all out the window. I couldn't think of anything witty to say. Where was Mae West when you needed her and that famous line, "Why don't you come up sometime and see me?" No, it was just me.

I didn't know how to shift my emotions from food to men.

I needed on-the-job training. What should I say when I looked into his dreamy eyes? Hug me now or forever hold your peace? *You have to have something in your repertoire!*

I wanted him to kiss me, but I couldn't figure out how to make it happen.

I wanted to feel his lips on mine.

I wanted to know what his lips tasted like on mine.

"Okay, hey, it's nice to met you. Thanks for the compliment."

I was surprised at the next words out of his mouth: "I would like to see you again. How about tomorrow night? It's Friday. Do you have any plans?"

Are you kidding me? The girls can walk the mall without me, for sure. But I had to play it cool.

I couldn't let him know I would be up all night wondering what to wear, how to fix my hair, whether I should change my nail polish. Should I shave—oh, of course, shave for sure.

"How about … well tomorrow sounds good. What time is good for you?"

Peter said, "How about right after work? We can do happy hour before dinner."

My girlfriends talked about how men are afraid of the *D* word—date. I wasn't going to say *it's a date*, for fear he would think I was rushing him. *Men like hanging out*—or at least that's what I had heard. Of course, I had to look like I knew what I was doing.

"Okay, then. I'll meet you here around five-thirty. Cool?"

"Yes," he said. "It's a date."

Never, ever, believe what your girlfriends say—especially if they have been on dates and you haven't been with them to see whether it's all true or not.

In all honesty, I didn't know what to do after that. Slowly, calmly, and in a rather sultry way, I said, "Okay, it's a date."

My palms were sweaty. I didn't know if my knees were knocking or had become locked together. What I did know was that I had a date with Peter. This would be my first real date as a thin woman.

Chapter 13

I couldn't believe I had never entered The Thai House from the main entrance. I always ordered my food for delivery or pickup. I was finally out of the house and with a man! When I arrived at the restaurant, the moment was a scene out of *Pretty Woman* with Julia Roberts and Richard Gere. Peter sat at the bar. I saw his reflection in the mirror behind the bar and our eyes met there first. He slowly turned around on the barstool and stood. He was so gallant, so tall. It was February in Florida and the weather was breezy. He was wearing a gold polo turtleneck with a black tweed blazer and black slacks. He looked like he'd had his hair cut; it was neat, short, black, and curly.

He was all of six feet two, and in heels, I was almost at his shoulder. He reached out to hug me; I tried not to fall into his arms. I felt cute but clumsy.

I rested my head directly on his chest. He slid his arms around my waist. I felt a tingle down my spine. He pulled me closer to him. I had not felt anything like this before. I don't think anyone had ever been able to get their arms around me. I felt safe, like nothing else mattered.

He pulled out the stool for me to sit. I watched him as he took off his jacket one arm at a time. My eyes scanned down the length of his body. Just like the movie *Jerry Maguire*—he had me at *hello.*

I couldn't remember anything my momma had told me. At this point, I couldn't remember who my momma was!

"Do you usually pick up women in restaurants?" I asked.

"Yes," he said. "If there is a woman I find attractive and I want to get to know her, I go for it. The place doesn't matter. Are you used to picking up strange men and going out to dinner with them?"

Okay, first of all, okay, okay ... stop! Your finger is in the air and your head is bobbing. Please don't embarrass us with that. Finger down slowly. Be still and just talk.

"Well, no, this is not my norm," I said as I motioned for the waiter. "Hi. May I have more lemon please?"

Good job! You played if off. I know this is all new for you, but you will find your way. Don't become someone else.

"You look amazing tonight," he said softly.

Okay, stop the planet. I want to get off! How often do you have a tall, cool-toned, mild-mannered Terence Howard say those words to you? I felt like I could go to heaven happy right then and there. Momma used to say, "When a man makes you feel something down there, cross your legs, and say no."

Then, it occurred to me—was he single? How would I know if he were single? This would not be the time to assume. I tried to think what my girlfriends would say now, but I couldn't. I had forgotten all about them.

After the second Diet Coke, the waiter showed us to the table. It was perfect—in a corner with an ocean view. The Thai House had an entrance from the pier.

"Wow, the view is spectacular."

"You mentioned this is your favorite place, but you only get the takeout on the other side. I thought I'd show you a better view."

Girl, he gets points for that!

We ordered food. I kept it real small not to give anything away. When the food arrived, I asked, "Hey, you want to pray over the food?"

"Sure," he said.

Girl, another point!

He said a few lines. It was short, an okay blessing. He didn't call down heaven or cast out demons or anything. That was cool. Peter ordered the special, and I ordered chicken pad thai. But I wanted to wet my appetite with Peter.

During dinner, I noticed him licking his lips between bites. Sensations in my body were awakened. Momma used to say ... *Girl, Momma always has something to say. Who* cares? *Who cares? She ain't here.*

"So, Peter, tell me, how do I get to know you?"

"Just ask," he said. "I'm an open book."

Let's try this out, I thought. I asked all sorts of questions. He was a pharmaceutical rep and very good at it. He went to school to be a pediatrician and then fell into his current position. He meditated to quiet his soul. I realized how much we had in common.

Talking to a real human and not a bucket of chicken every night was much more interesting. Peter had one more drink, and I had another Diet Coke for the road. He sipped his drink, and I enjoyed the atmosphere and view.

"I'd rather be somewhere with you sitting next to me, laying your head against my chest, just relaxing," he said.

Okay, if I am already in heaven, where do I go from here?

I smiled and said, "It's almost that time."

"Time for what?

"I should be getting home. I have an early morning."

"Okay. No problem."

The valet brought the car around. A girlfriend from work had dropped me at the restaurant, so I got to see what kind of car he drove. It was very nice, clean, and still had the new-car smell. On the ride home, soft jazz played on the radio.

We arrived at my apartment. He came around and opened the door for me. He began to walk me to the door. I said, "It's okay. You don't have to walk me up."

Okay, who said that? Momma, is that you?

I knew I didn't want the night to end, and I most definitely didn't want to be alone. But I was too afraid. Why did the fear lift its ugly head? When would it go away?

I stood there at the base of the steps looking into Peter's eyes. *Is this real? What do I do? There is no way this man could be real.*

"Can I kiss you good night?" Peter whispered.

Girl, a gentleman!

He slowly leaned in, placed both his hands on my cheeks, and gently touched my lips with his. So sweet, it was the cutest peck. I didn't move away when it was over. Here was my opportunity to finally taste his lips. I slowly slid my tongue toward his lips just to get a hint, and his tongue met mine. His lips didn't taste or smell like fried chicken.

The kiss was amazing! I couldn't deny it.

"It's been a wonderful night," I said softly. "Thank you so much. I really had a great time. I didn't know we had so much in common."

"I hope it's only the beginning," Peter said.

I smiled, hugged him, and walked up the stairs toward the lobby door.

I entered the door to my apartment. My phone rang. It was Peter. "Hey, you going to be up for a few minutes?" he asked.

"I'm running a bath. I have a few minutes to chat while you are on your way home."

"I find you so easy to talk to," he said.

No one had ever said that to me before.

It was two forty-five in the morning before the call ended. Time flew.

I knew where his parents were born and raised. How many brothers and sisters he had. Where he went to school. How many gifts he bought at Christmas for nieces and nephews. Wow, he had a family. *I could have a family.*

After we said goodnight, thoughts of insecurity and fear crept in. I couldn't sleep.

What if it wasn't enough?

If I cherished the moments, would that be enough?

Panic set in.

I felt like a fish out of water.

I didn't know where to go from there.

I felt inept.

I needed something sweet, crunchy, fried, broiled, grilled. Box, bag, tray, slab.

I stopped myself. I couldn't imagine anything tasting as good as this moment felt right now.

Peter was the reason I felt so good.

He was the reason I didn't eat.

The talks and dates with Peter continued. There were attempts at intimacy. But I shot them down. I was scared to death. It was all new to me.

Peter was funny, attractive, and intelligent. He was a successful professional. I didn't have to pay for anything, although I did on occasion. It was only fair.

I thought, *Could he be the one? But, does he know he's the one?*

If he didn't know it, it didn't matter. My sister always said a man has to be attracted to you first and want you more, or everything is moot.

Chapter 14

I was treading lightly, cautiously, and Peter was full-steam ahead. We went to movies, dinner, theatre, and the ballet. Peter invited me on weekend trips. The fear of intimacy had me stuck. I made excuse after excuse. It had been nine months, and all I would say was, "No, thank you," or "that's too much." "It's such a huge gift that there's no way I can accept it."

We were at dinner one night at my favorite restaurant—The Thai House—at a table looking out at the ocean. We were almost a year strong.

After finishing a wonderful dinner, Peter asked, "Hey, what do you think about us going to the Virgin Islands for a weekend?"

"When?" I asked.

"Well, if I tell you which weekend, you will come up with an excuse. How about I surprise you? What's wrong? What's the matter? Have I done something to you to make you feel uncomfortable? Am I moving too fast?" Peter inquired.

"Well, now that you mention it," I started, "yes, you are moving faster than I am used to."

Used to? Girl, when was the last time you were invited to the Virgin Islands? You better get it straight and give the man what he wants.

"What makes you afraid?" he whispered.

In this moment, I was burning up. I looked down into my glass, watching the ice melt in my Diet Coke, wishing I could rub a piece of it on the back of my neck. I slowly lifted my head, looked directly into his eyes, and said softly, "I honestly don't know."

"Well, maybe we can figure it out together." He reached across the table and took my hand in his.

I had never heard that from a man.

Girl, how many times are you going to stop what comes naturally? You two are both consenting adults! Give him some! He deserves it!

"How do we do that?" I asked.

"Well," he hesitated. Again, I found my head down and my eyes on the ice.

I saw his left hand come toward my face slowly and gently. He placed his two fingers under my chin, gently lifted my head, and said, "We can talk about it whenever, wherever, for as long as you want."

He reached over the table and kissed me softly on the lips. I leaned back in my chair, and he sat back in his. "Don't move," I whispered. "I need to freeze-frame and capture you, all of you!"

He smiled and said, "It's real. It's happening."

I thought, *You can't make this stuff up. He must have been a psychiatrist in another life. He is reading me too well.*

Girl, if I told you once, I told you twice—if you want to keep him, you are going to have to have sex with him.

But there has to be more than that. That is not enough.

"Give it up," I said under my breath.

"Give what up?" Peter choked on his drink.

"Did you hear me?" I asked.

"Yes. I'm looking at the menu and asking you what you feel like tonight. I meant *what do you want to eat for dinner*, and you said 'give it up!'"

We both laughed.

"So, you want to tell me what that's all about?"

"Nope," I snapped back, "discussion not necessary."

"Wow, you are so mysterious. It keeps me intrigued."

"Is that a bad thing?"

"No, it turns me on to be honest," Peter said with a big grin on his face.

I giggled.

We finished dinner and arrived at my place. "You might as well park and come up for a few," I said.

His eyes widened with a smile that challenged the sun. I abruptly said, "Calm down. It's just for a few minutes, not all night. You get it?"

"Yes, yes, I get it. I can do a few minutes—and all night. We can talk all night long. I am up for it."

The expression on my face spoke for itself: *Yeah, right! Yeah, sure, buddy, you would talk all night.*

Believe it or not, that's exactly what we did. I threw a blanket on the floor in front of the sofa and served a bowl of popcorn and soda. *When Harry Met Sally* was on the TV. Peter hit the mute button and said, "Okay, go ahead. Talk."

"No way! What do you mean 'talk'? We're watching the movie."

"No. *You* were watching the movie. I want to hear more about you." He shifted further down on the blanket. He propped his head up on his right hand, widened his eyes, and waited.

"Uh, I am not sure what you mean," I said.

"Oh, don't play shy. I know you want to talk."

"Okay, yes. I want to, but you first."

He started with his college days. How he wished he'd chosen another career. Peter was a pharmaceutical rep, but he wanted to be a pediatric physician. He loved working with children, but he'd moved his way up the ladder in pharmaceuticals. He got caught up in the politics of the job and attached to the money and status. "Now I feel dead on the inside. When I was in med school, I did an internship at a children's hospital and felt alive when I was there—like I had purpose." He rolled over on his back, folded his hands behind his head, and stared at the ceiling.

Wow. I have to say something profound. Deeply interesting—no, captivating. "I never heard anyone express that money and prestige left them feeling empty."

Ok, girl, he's gonna head for the door; you just blew it!

"I know. I never thought I could say it out loud. BJ, you are easy to talk to."

He leaned over and kissed me.

There was no saving me now. I was gone. *Man down!* I was captured. I knew it and so did he. He pulled me on top of him. He gently touched my lips, and the taste of his tongue excited me. He exhaled; I inhaled. I breathed him into me. The rest of my body wanted him, needed him. The kiss felt like it lasted for an hour.

Girl, you better start saying the Lord's Prayer. "Our *Father, who art in heaven …*" My mind had gone blank! *Oh, no. I can't remember the Lord's Prayer. I am going to hell.*

I gently pulled our lips apart, leaned back, resting on the palms of my hands, and looked at him.

"Are you okay?" he said.

"I have to pee," I said. *Thank goodness for small bladders.*

"Are you sure?" he groaned.

"Well, I think I should know when I have to pee." With a deep sigh, he began to release the grip around my waist and butt. *Another near miss.* I returned from the bathroom. Peter was sitting on the sofa with the volume turned up on the TV. The night came to a close.

That didn't stop Peter. He offered to whisk me away to another romantic destination. I had met Peter after the first of this year, and now we were heading toward the fall. He asked me again to go to the islands.

We'd seen each other at least three days a week and almost every other weekend. Honestly, I couldn't go. I had a preplanned trip to see my mother. It wasn't an excuse.

It was 8:00 p.m. on the Friday night before I was planning to leave to go see Mom. My cell phone rang. It was Peter.

"I just want to give it one more try. Are you sure I can't take you away this weekend?"

A huge smile covered my face.

"Peter, where are you?"

"Five minutes away from you," he said.

"Well, I have to finish packing. I leave early in the morning. I will see you when I return. Be safe."

We both knew why he was five minutes away— another attempt at intimacy. I couldn't risk it.

I arrived at the airport at five in the morning on Saturday to learn that my flight departed Friday morning, not Saturday. I had missed my flight, and the airline was booked. I couldn't get another flight.

I immediately called my mother.

"Well, honey, I thought you said you were coming yesterday," she said, "and when you didn't show, I just figured, well, there goes my mind again, and you would get here when you could."

"Mom, I am so sorry," I said, almost in tears.

We were both so looking forward to seeing each other; I couldn't believe I'd made a mistake like that.

Did I really want Peter to take me away?

Not at the expense of not seeing my mother … or did I?

Decide what to do. I went back to the airport parking lot, found my car, and started home. *I'll get some takeout and go home. Sounds like a plan.*

I arrived at The Thai House, picked up my usual order, and went home.

I called Peter to explain what had happened, but the call went into voicemail. This went on for two weeks. I left messages and texts, but still I couldn't reach Peter.

Chapter 15

I began to worry. I made one last effort to contact Peter. I texted him: "Hi, I'm trying to reach you. I just want to know you're okay, or should I call the police just in case? Please respond to let me know you are okay."

An hour or so later I received a text that read, "Hi, all is well. I am sorry for the disconnect. All the best."

Okay, what just happened?

Did I just get dumped?

Did I just get dumped with a text message?

Wait a minute. Let's regroup what's going on?

He approached me, right? Right?

He asked me out, right? Right? So what the … What just happened?

I wanted to be sure he was okay. I sent another text that read, "Hey, are you sure you're okay."

Okay, are you stalking him now?

Did I do or say something wrong?

Can we talk about it?

There was no response for days. Day-in and day-out, I checked my phone—no calls, no text.

Just as Peter entered my life, he was no longer there.

But I couldn't disconnect just like that.

I couldn't let it go.

I realized I had feelings that I'd never had for another person before. They were real, and they hurt.

I was in my kitchen looking out the window. I heard his voice; I felt his touch.

In a moment, my body went numb.

I couldn't feel anything. I wanted to die. I ran to my bedroom, crawled into bed, rolled up into a ball, and pulled a blanket over my head.

I wasn't hungry, but food thoughts were coming fast and furious. Cakes, cookies, and ice cream filled my head. Whole pizzas, cheese steaks and fries, a half a ham with mac and cheese would really hit the spot.

If I ate now, I knew I wouldn't stop for three or four days—maybe even a week. I would bleed out. Was it worth it. Why?

Order a dozen pizzas—one large pizza with sausage pepperoni, onions, mushrooms, and bell peppers—with chips and dip on the side. Gallons of Chinese House fried rice and chicken and broccoli could help.

No, get three whole submarines, one with turkey and cheese, the other Italian salami, pepperoni, spicy ham, and Swiss cheese with extra onions. That would do the trick! Oh, oh, oh, carrot cake and vanilla ice cream—that's it!

There was nothing on the planet that could make me feel any better or relieve the pain I was in.

It was 2:00 a.m. I moved to the space where Peter and I had sat and talked all night and almost ... *Wow, it could have ... it could have happened. Then what?*

What just happened? Did he owe me an explanation? *No!*

Sure, he does.

Are you crazy? You almost ...

What if I did?

Say it!

I can't.

Say it!

Okay, I almost had sex with him.

It doesn't count if you hadn't planned it.

Who says that? What about now? What do I do?

Oh, Girl, please, you are not the only woman that's been dumped. It's been going on for years.

Was I dumped? He didn't say that.

You are not the first and certainly not the last.

It was not okay. I really liked him.

You should have had sex when I told you to. But not you, you are here crying alone, wanting to eat everything in the kitchen, or worse.

Our Father who art in heaven, help me!

Now you remember the prayer. Go figure.

Chapter 16

Sunday, 2:30 p.m. I was still in the fetal position. I hadn't moved from where I was Saturday night.

How do you speak anguish?

How do you communicate despair?

What comes after being empty? Nothing!

Should I call him again?

The light had gone out in my soul.

The food thoughts were there, but I was more afraid of throwing up, or worse. I couldn't eat a thing. *So, this is how the skinny girls stay thin.*

I checked the volume on my phone. I couldn't understand why Peter didn't call.

I placed the phone back on the floor face down.

I looked at the pictures of my girlfriends and family on the wall. We had a great time at barbecues, holiday parties, baby showers, weddings.

I have a life. I have a family and friends who love me. How did I end up here wanting to die?

I crawled to the bathroom and looked at myself in the minor. "What's wrong with me? Why?" I asked.

No answer.

I stepped in front of the full-length mirror in my bedroom to see all of me. I was now half my former size.

I was the skinny girl.

I looked like *that* girl. Why did this happen?

Was this supposed to happen to a skinny girl?

I wanted to be *that* girl. The girl everyone wants.

Tears filled my eyes and ran down my face. I put my head in my hands, crawled into bed, pulled the cover over my head, and stayed there.

Monday night at 9:00 p.m., the doorbell rang. I sat straight up in the bed.

I couldn't remember where I was.

My pillow was tear-soaked and smeared with mascara. My eyes were burning from the tears. The bell rang again.

Okay, okay, it's him. It's Peter—finally. He's come to talk and tell me all about what happened. Why he couldn't talk. Is it family, a friend? It would be okay if he told me he has a girlfriend. I just need to see him.

I got out of bed and ran to the intercom. I pressed the bottom. "Yes, who is it?" I was so tired I could hardly speak. "Yes, who is it?"

"Hi. Is Cynthia in?" The voice asked.

"Wrong apartment. Ring 3G."

I walked away from the intercom and back to bed.

It was 1:00 a.m. I woke up and set the alarm clock. I'd taken a vacation day on Monday, but Tuesday I had to get to work.

The alarm sounded and woke me up at eight thirty. *Really?* I set the clock for eight thirty instead of six thirty. *Great, so now I can just call in sick. Did I do that on purpose?*

I couldn't face anybody right then. With all the crying, my body felt like it had hit a Mack Truck. My brain was a blank computer screen. Everything did not compute. My brain was fried.

Hey, I got a great idea. Let's go get some breakfast. IHOP is down the street; you can call in a pickup order. Don't hash browns sound good? Oh, how about grits?

Okay, listen. You sound off the wall. Food ain't love, and it sure can't help you now.

Just call it in.

There's no way I can put that amount of food in my body the way I feel. What the? Why am I being tormented with food again?

You don't want to talk to him. What else do we do? There has to be another way.

I got dressed and put makeup my face so I wouldn't look like the scarecrow from the *Wizard of Oz*. I was headed to IHOP.

I got in my car and drove off. I put in a CD and turned the volume up past sixty. I didn't want to hear anything, but I couldn't stop the moans of my soul. I was aching. What could I do?

Chapter 17

I wanted to hate him.

But I didn't know how.

I wanted to be angry at him.

But I couldn't let myself.

I had a life that felt right. *Right?*

I was no longer in the house having a relationship with food. I was alive.

I had a reason to live.

I no longer missed food.

I talked to Peter, he talked back.

For the first time, I knew what love felt like, and then it went away. I wanted it back. *Was it real?*

Food is the only thing that is real.

Who said that?

It was that first kiss that turned on all the colors in the garden and everything was bright and vibrant.

I could actually see and express how I felt on the inside. I didn't feel the fear. Anything outside of fear was wonderful.

Before Peter, I didn't know flowers had different scents—some sweet, some captivating, others thick and heady, still others light and whimsical. I didn't know smells outside of the aromas from food.

I didn't know men had a smell, which smells really good, as a matter of fact.

I didn't know that if I stood real close I could hear his heart beat.

I had heard Peter's heart, and it sounded beautiful.

I told him he had a rhythm all his own. There were times I would lay my head on his chest with my fingers on the front of my neck trying to catch his beat—to see if our hearts really beat as one. I had heard it in a movie, but now I knew it doesn't really work.

When we walked through the park, he leaned against a tree and hugged me. I laid my head on his chest, he wrapped his arms all the way around me, and I felt safe. When I closed my eyes, sometimes I could still feel his arms around me and hear his heartbeat.

"Squeeze tighter," I would ask him, and he would. I felt clothed in warmth and safety. No one, *no one*, could ever hurt me.

I would tell him, "Don't let go."

He'd say, "Never. I will never let you go."

I wanted him. He was a part of me. There was an ache inside of me.

How did I let this happen?

How did he get in?

Did it start when I let go of the food? In my mind, I loved my life with food. No pain, tragedy, or despair.

I didn't feel alone with food. I was safe. Then, I opened up to give love a chance.

Love don't live here no more. I don't think it ever will again.

It had been months, and I hadn't spoken to Peter. I had moments when I wanted to call him and ask him *why? What happened?* But I didn't.

Chapter 18

Nothing could beat Christmas in New York. I worked in NYC as a paralegal. Holiday parties at law firms were the event of the year. You'd mix and mingle with the firm's top clients. I'd worked for firms managing client accounts such as *The New York Times*, Chase, Wells Fargo, Sandoz Pharmaceuticals, Dean Witter—the list went on. You rubbed elbows with the *rainmakers*—those ten-million-dollar men and their special clients. The location had to be upscale and elegant to impress. It was a red-carpet event, a not-to-be missed black-tie affair. Ten-foot Christmas trees and elaborate decorations filled the floor. The firm had taken it to the nines, renting out the entire second floor of a hotel. The limos pulled up out front as photographers snapped end-of-the-year pictures.

There were long, short, midlength, and minidresses of all shapes and sizes. The ladies pulled out all the stops. Who would guess that after a couple of eggnogs, you could meet Mr. Right Now at a holiday party? It took a month to find the perfect dress. I started to shop in October.

This was my coming-out party. The dress I found was twelve sizes smaller than I had ever worn to one of these events. I couldn't believe the surgery had been five years earlier. There were thirteen of us in the stretch limo, someone from each department. Everyone exited the limo. I was the last one. I sat there with my legs crossed (the first time I didn't need one person on each knee pushing together). I felt like Cinderella. This was my moment.

Tonight was the night, and I was going to make it mine.

The driver peeked in and asked, "Are you ready?"

"Yes," I said. He held my hand as I exited. The photographer was snapping my year-end photo. I heard my name being called, but I couldn't see anyone as I walked up the red carpet.

"Work it, girl! Work that thang!" It was Sergio, the paralegal from Trust and Estates. I started to giggle and

wave. Sergio didn't compliment anybody. I felt alive.
I was standing at the entrance of the hotel in a black
Evan-Picone cocktail dress with sequined bodice and
black sequined shawl, off–black, ultra-sheer stockings,
and open-toed sandals with three-inch heels. I felt
good, and it showed on the outside.

"You look beautiful, girl," Sergio slurred, sounding
drunk already. He grabbed my hand and whispered,
"Come on, girl, let's drink!"

"Are you sure? It sounds like you had enough.
What time did you get here?"

"Girl, I started at happy hour. You late," he giggled.

It was now eight thirty, and he was hammered but
still standing.

"My limo driver is the designated driver. I came
prepared. It's free," he stammered and belched.

I proceeded to the buffet and picked up a small
saucer. *Play it safe, and slowly eat your way through this
one.* I piled it high. I started eating off the plate before
I sat down.

*Girl, here I am. What the! Why are you stuffing your
face with food? You are the hottest thing here. Go find you
a million-dollar man and have a dance. When we get home
I refuse to listen to you cry and moan about how much food*

you ate. You don't want to end up in the emergency room tonight?

She was back. I had just placed the fourth shrimp cocktail on my plate and thought, *Let's get another one.* I felt a tap on my shoulder. I thought it was Sergio.

"Sergio, I—"

"Hello, BJ," he said. I placed the saucer on the table and stepped back. I slowly lifted my head and inhaled. *Oh, yes. Girl, it's him. Whatcha gonna do now?*

He stood there smiling with those beautiful hazel eyes. "You look amazing!" he said.

"Hello, Peter. Why are you here?"

"My company moved here two years ago, and they have a holiday party here every year. We have the entire first floor of the hotel," he said.

Oh, Humphrey Bogart, take me away, "Out of all the gin joints in the world you had to walk into mine."

Hello! Come back, girl. Say something.

"Okay, it's nice seeing you," I said. I began to turn away.

"Are you here with someone, BJ?"

"No."

He put both his hands on my shoulders and massaged them like he used to do and said "Come on, don't be like that. It's Christmas."

When his hand touched my shoulder, my knees started shaking and my stomach quivered.

I still couldn't resist. I wasn't over him. Time heals all wounds, but it hadn't been long enough.

Girl, go ahead, have a drink with him. The only thing that could happen is, well, what almost happened before.

"Peter, it is awesome to see you, but I have to spread some holiday cheer. Be good to yourself."

I held my breath.

I walked away, leaving Peter standing at the buffet table. I proceeded to the food in the next room. I wolfed down four shrimp puffs and headed for the bar. Still chewing, I asked the bartender, "What goes good with shrimp?"

"I have a great Pinot Grigio."

"Okay, let's do it." Before I knew it, I had drunk three glasses of wine and then scurried back over to the buffet table and heaved in another four shrimp.

The last thing I wanted to do was get drunk at a holiday party. I refused to be the talk of the firm.

I searched out Sergio. I found him crunched in a corner in a cozy chair by the fireplace, sleeping off the booze.

I shook him. "Sergio, Sergio, wake up!" I whispered. I didn't want anyone to see me waking him up.

"What?"

"It's time to go. I need a ride home in your limo. Come on, take me home. I don't feel well."

If he had known the real reason I had to leave, I would have never heard the end of it. Sergio was one of those *love 'em and leave 'em* guys. His heart had hardened from all the disappointment and betrayal relationships can bring.

I called for his limo driver. It took about fifteen minutes for him to come. We were waiting at the door for the limo, and Peter walked over to me with a champagne flute in each hand and said gently, passionately, "Let's toast Christmas together and to a wonderful new year for us."

Sergio woke up when he heard Peter's voice.

"No!" Sergio yelled. "I know who you are, and you better leave my girl alone. You broke her heart one time! You don't get a second chance."

"Wow, so you talk about me, huh?" Peter scoffed.

"Oh, not anymore. There *were* days. Today is a new day. Whatever the reason for you not returning my calls, take it with you now and don't call me. And trust me, I won't call you."

Girl, why did you have to tell Serg? He runs his mouth like a woman. Sometimes I think he is a woman. But he's just a little too much girlfriend tonight.

"Sergio, I got this," I said. The car arrived. "Get in the car, Serg." I grabbed a flute from Peter's hand and gulped the champagne. It was my fourth glass. I leaned into him and gave him a big, wet kiss. "Thanks for the lesson. I learned a lot," I said.

I walked to the limo and didn't look back.

Chapter 19

∞

"One drink is enough to feel the effects of the alcohol." That's what the assistant said before the surgery. One drink was never enough for someone like me.

There was no stopping. The cage was open. The dragon was free. I had a problem. I was not a successful drinker. But I didn't know that.

I left the party with Sergio in tow. I stopped at the nearest liquor store for a couple of bottles of chardonnay.

I didn't blame it on the alcohol. I wanted it.

I decided, *I'll take the safe way. I'll drink my way through life for the next few years.* Boy, was I wrong.

For fifteen years or more after that one party, I experienced periods of uncontrollable drinking, along with huge consequences—geographical changes, broken relationships, loss of employment, family turmoil. No jail time, thank God, but *life completely out of control.*

What was going on?

I was that girl. I was one of the girls now. You know—the girl the guys look at and say, "Girl, you look so good I could sop you up wit' a biscuit."

Where had I gone? Instead of stuffing my face with food, I was drowning my pain with booze.

The booze masked my feelings until I was well past the brink. *What now?*

I needed to find something to stop the feelings. Drinking was not the answer.

Chapter 20

Moment of Clarity

I didn't know I was depressed. I didn't want to do anything. I couldn't focus. I was lethargic, listless. I couldn't think. I didn't want to give up my relationship with food.

You didn't miss a chapter.

I returned to what I knew.

What made me feel comfortable.

What was easy and familiar.

I know it sounds crazy, but in my mind, food was my friend. I chose to run to it when life got hard.

I couldn't process or rationalize the fact that I lived in fear and torment from my past.

The only way out was to run.

I knew where drinking would take me—back to where I'd already been. I refused to go back there.

But food ... I could eat and drive. I wouldn't get pulled over for eating a three-piece on 95N.

I could close down the buffet.

I could eat my way through town and still walk the white line.

When I saw myself, food was what I did.

It was all I did—eat.

Stress? Grab a bag.

Depressed? Grab a box.

Angry? Grab a slab.

There had to be something outside of this vicious cycle.

As a child, I had been helpless. As an adult, I made choices that were not the best. I no longer had to live out what had been imposed on me.

Food failed me. It was not a solution.

I was seeking comfort when I needed a solution— an active, practical solution to the problem.

I ran from my feelings. I ran to food.

I ate volumes of food to pass out, due to emotions I didn't want to experience again. I couldn't handle the feelings.

The experiences were in my head; the emotions I couldn't address for fear they would overwhelm me.

What was it about me that I didn't want to face?

Why did I run to food for cover?

What was truly on the other side? *Freedom and Peace.*

I was at the end of self. No pride, no ego, no more excuses. Did I really have to look at me?

What would I see?

What was haunting me?

What was it I didn't want to feel?

This was my wake-up call. I made a decision that could affect the rest of my life.

The pain on the inside was unbearable.

I was back in the bed in the fetal position.

New town. New apartment. New life, but *same old stuff.*

The apartment was quiet and before the dream began I said ...

"God can you hear me? I'm begging you to help me. Please, I can't give up food. It's all I have. You don't

understand. I need it. I really do! I will be a good Christian, I promise. I will love my neighbor. I will give an offering. Please, I don't know how to love you more than I love the food. I can't let you take the place of food. It hurts too much! You don't understand. I don't know how to give up food. I don't know how to live without it. I don't know how to love you. Food is safe. I've heard you are a God of judgment, a hell-fire and brimstone God. If don't get it right, I go to hell. I get whacked whenever I screw up. I screw up, that's it—game over. For all I know, my life is this way because of you. You made me this way."

When my siblings and I were kids, my mom read Bible verses to us. She made us repeat them after her.

At my lowest point, I could hear, "The Lord is my shepherd" (Psalm 23 NLT). I began to weep.

I didn't know why I was crying or if anybody could hear me, but again in my head I heard Mom say …

"You can trust His word."

"But in my distress I cried out to the LORD; yes, I cried to my God for help. He heard me from his sanctuary; my cry reached his ears." (2 Samuel 22:7 NLT).

I let go of the biggest cry I could muster and said, "God, if you are real, you have to help me. Help me. Help me, please. I'm not going to make it. Everything is so messed up. I can't get it right. I don't want to do this anymore. Life is too hard. I thought I had love, but its not. I live life numbing my emotions."

Suddenly, I heard a voice sounding like mine, but it came from the inside of me.

"Trust me to heal you," the voice said.

"That's a lot to ask," I said.

Okay, wait, who are you talking to?

Is that God? I'm I talking to God? He really does talk back?

He does show up—and talks back.

Me, the biggest sinner ever. How can this be?

I thought you had to be perfect and all righteous for God to acknolwedge you.

Okay, now since the communication lines are open, I have some stuff to say.

"Wait, BJ. Stop and think. Are you crazy?" I say. "Are you really going to talk to God and say real stuff? Not just recite the Lord's Prayer or ask Him for stuff you don't believe you can get anyway? Is that what you are about to do?"

I made a decision within myself: This was my time. I had to do something different because the same old stuff wasn't working anymore.

Okay, God, here we go.

"You put these people in my life, and they hurt me. How can I trust you?" I asked.

"My life is this way because of you." I shouted.

First, I looked up for thunder or lightning or God whacking me with a tree or a house. The apartment didn't blow up. Nothing.

It was still and quiet.

"You made your choices of your own free will. I had nothing to do with them," God said.

I can barely explain what happened from that moment on. I felt peace.

Before I knew it, I was pouring my heart out to God.

Did I just encounter God, for real?

What day is it?

What time is it?

I checked my watch. It was the same day and not much time had past.

It is true: "A single day in your courts is better than a thousand anywhere else!" (Psalm 84:10 NLT).

How did He know?

Was He there the whole time?

I was born again and had been for years, but I'd never opened up to God.

Somehow I connected God to my real dad. I thought their characters were somehow the same. Could it be that the word *father* threw me?

I didn't think He cared.

I really didn't think He answered.

Boy, slap me with surprise. This is *the Father God.*

I asked God the one question you are not supposed to ask: *Why?*

Why did you let all this happen to me?

I didn't hear a voice, but inside of me I began to understand.

There were people in my life who made choices out of their own free will. God didn't let or make them do anything. He had nothing to do with *their* choices.

Wow! Why did I understand that now? Why did it take so long for me to get it?

I realized I had spent too much time blaming God. I could see now it was not His fault.

People make choices.

The circumstances that had occurred in my life were because of the choices I had made.

Today, I have morning talks with God, and I read His Word daily.

The more I talk, the easier it gets.

I also found a new way of talking—and that's by not talking.

I listen. I know, a new concept for me too!

I express my fear and inadequacy.

I recognize it's through my spirit God speaks to me. He always guides me to a book or verse in His Word, and I see the answer right there.

Today, I set a time aside daily to journal. I want to get to the core of *why* and *what*. I pray and ask God for clarity, wisdom, and direction.

I make an inventory of my life and the exact nature of *why, what,* and *how.*

I take responsibility for my mistakes and forgive those who harm me.

It's a process, but worthwhile.

Today, I can face whatever comes my way because I have the tools to process any situation.

I let go of the losses of my past and embrace what awaits me. And the journey continues.

Printed in the United States
By Bookmasters

Printed in the United States
By Bookmasters